"12 months from Now"

BOOK II

…a chronicle of my 4th Church Assignment

SIR FINIS DeMILO BREWER

(SIR…the "SOUL"man)

12 Months From Now/Book II

12 Months From Now/Book II

Copyright 2015

By: SIR FINIS DeMILO BREWER

Published by:

TOOSWEETPUBLISHING productions
P.O. Box 6512 New Orleans, Louisiana
70174   Website:
TOOSWEETPUBLISHING.COM
email: toosweetpublishing@yahoo.com

ISBN: 978-0-941091-16-9

ALL RIGHTS RESERVED. No part of this book can be reproduced in any form, without the written permission of the Publisher.

First Printing

PRINTED IN THE UNITED STATES OF AMERICA

12 Months From Now/Book II

Heavenly Father,

let not my heart grow weary

And let not my faith in YOU,

ever fail;

And let my trust be in you always,

And not in Man

As I journey on this "straight & narrow"

Trail.

SIR

7-16-2003/8:50am

Wednesday Night Bible Study …September 18, 2013

Well… I'm trying to hurry up and finish this entry while the "residual anointing "still rest upon me.

Phew!

I'm so tired though; I actually dozed off while the Laptop rebooted itself. I guess I better wake-up and get to writing.

Bible Study was ok. I was expecting the "belong groups" to meet tonight but I guess my schedule is still out of sync. I'm still trying to figure it all out, but I guess if you miss a couple of Sunday's & Wednesday nights (like I have), you'll be clueless (like I am) to what's really going on. I'm trying to keep up, but my personal life is just crap right now. Don't know where my daughters are; ex have lost her "damn" mind; I'm living with friends(again); lost everything (again) that I worked for; can't even call my job a job; and definitely can't call my paycheck pay or a check...it's more like legalized pimping by the state of Texas.

When I work a full week, (which I haven't in weeks) I take home $170.00, and the "slime=bucket of a lying lawyer" got the state of Texas taking $250.00 every week. What's wrong with that picture? Do the math...(lying slime dog of a lawyer). Well, I digress... (again)...sorry.

I'm trying to write this entry while it's still fresh in my mind, because I really don't like when I have to play "catch-up". This is Book II, and it was suppose to start with last Sunday's service (which was sooo good) but I just couldn't get the moment to write it all down. After the "Holy Spirit" lead me to end Book I now, and use last Sunday's service as the start of Book II, I had to re-group. So I re-grouped.

I went to Bible Study tonight with a lot expectations, and I guess I didn't get them all fulfilled. The sermon started in the Book of Genesis…wait…I'm trying to remember… (pause)…I got it! The 39th Chapter starting at the first verse where the subject was referring to Joseph and how GOD had favored & blessed everything he put his hands to do in the house of the Egyptian as a slave. It was good teaching, and of course I was quite familiar with the subject. But from the looks of the Bible I was using, you'd think I just walked out the store with it. My personal Bible(s) are all written in, highlighted, and lots of evidence of "wear & tear". I feel so lost when I don't have them, and I'm forced to use someone else's. Everything I own is either packed in one play sister's shed, another play sister's closet, and the rest stuffed beyond capacity in my '99 Blue Suburban (that I love sitting on 22" inch rims) parked in the driveway of the play sister's house where the packed shed is. I don't sleep at this location because there were out-of-town house guest in attendance…Unexpected house guest to both of us.

The houses that we both were individually trying to buy never happened. We never saw the inside of the Title company for the real estate closing. The jerk (John Labee) turned out to be a scam artist. Taking people money, say they are going to close on such & such date, and never close on the property. Tells hundreds of Lies, and feel no shame. Towards the end of our "never-happen" closing, he was arrested by the Slidell Police and indicted on federal charges of Tax Fraud. Look it up!...we couldn't believe it ourselves.

My play sister Angela got her money returned (minus $120.00); she is still waiting for the latter. I'm still waiting for my $1750.00 he owes me, and he have lied at least a hundred times about that...but that's another story too. But I better change the subject cause I'm about to get angry all over again.

So I guess since we were supposed to be in our own houses, her son (my lovely "play nephew") KT, had friends schedule to fly in from L.A. for the "Animate Fest" that was being held in September. Well when they arrived, it was the first week of August. So to give them the room that three guys would need to stretch out, I opt to go by my other "play Sister" Jackie. Her daughter (my god-child) stays at her MaMa's with her "mama Gwen", so her room was offered to me. So I took her up on the offer; I've been here every since. Of course my being homeless is not by choice; it's just the side-effect of SIN…adultery, fornication, Lies, you name it…Really caught me by surprise.

The "out-of-town" guest at Angela's house left a few days ago, and it has taken its toll on her. I guess it was not explained to my naïve nephew that if you invite guest to visit, 4 weeks is a bit much. I'm sure he has learned his lesson from his Mother, and I'm sure it was not an easy lesson to endure. I've experience a few of her "talks". The yelling, cussing, and her rather un-petite size, I think it's easier to just "go to jail" than take her tongue lashings…LOL (love ya Sis).

I'm sure many wonder about all these "play sisters" that I have; well I got real ones also. They love ME just as much…even more so (if it was possible. I'm just a pretty loveable brother that knows how to fix almost anything. My ex-wife never understood the affection that I show my sister's when I see them, but she just dizzy like that. I didn't grow up in a house where people cuss, fuss, and drink all day. Or a house where people thought hugging your brother was "gay"…she was just dizzy. No affection toward each other is the world she grew up in. I LOVE my Sisters (and they LOVE their Brother), and I'm going to always show them. The older they get, the more I LOVE them…and that's that.

So all my "stuff" is between Fort Worth, Texas and New Orleans, Louisiana. (I so love being back HOME in New Orleans; thank you LORD JESUS!). Spread between several locations between both states; it's my Life at the moment.

I was talking to GOD today on my way to church, and I gave him an update on my life, in case my file got misplaced. Well actually, I told JESUS since that is the proper protocol For the Bible says,

"no man comes to the Father except through the Son").

So I said to JESUS, "LORD, sometimes I wonder if I did somebody something to cause all this "madness" in my life".

I didn't drink (never been drunk); didn't cuss (said the "F" word for the first time while telling a joke 25 years ago); didn't fool around(stayed faithful while married even though they didn't); and just always treated people nice.

So I said,

"LORD…WHAT THE HELL HAPPEN!"

Yea I was mad, but I still was respectful (we ARE talking about Daddy GOD).

So as I was riding across the GNO heading to Bible Study, I got a revelation. I said,

"LORD, ..I mean… LORD JESUS, if you died on the Cross for all my sins, then there is nothing I could have said, done, or thought that would justify & warrant all that has happen to me."

Then I added,

"So if that is the case, SOMEBODY owes me! The Word of GOD says if satan steals something from you, then he has to restore it; seven fold. Soooo, I am due a payday!"

As I thought along these lines, I thought about when "JOB" Life was turned upside down. The Bible says that,

"…the LORD gave "JOB" twice as much as he had before" (Job 42:10).

And it also says in verse 12,

"So the LORD blessed the latter end of "JOB" more than his beginning…"

So I pondered the thought,

"Who is gonna replace and/or restore all that has been lost over the past 19 years of my life...If I only counting the ministry era?

"Who LORD JESUS?"

I know growing up we were taught not to question GOD (another one of those "big Lies" satan fooled us with), but I ask GOD questions all the time. And this was one question I needed to know the answer to.

It took me about 20 minutes to get to church, and I made sure to pick up the recorded message from Sunday. This will be the very first message that I've purchased from the ministry, and I'm looking forward to listening to it.

(Ummm…I could play it in my Laptop right now while I'm typing. Nope, better not; that would be just asking for trouble).

I bought this Laptop at a pawn shop for $89.00 dollars, and it has been such a blessing to have. It has helped me with a lot of my writing projects. But I shouldn't ask more of it than it's capable of delivering; it's not a top of the line "Acer" purchased from "Best Buy", but it's getting the job done.

Sometimes like our equipment, we should tell ourselves, "stay in ya lane bro…Stay…in… your…Lane!" And not get over our heads. The two computers I did purchase from "Best Buy" cost me over $1200 dollars in 2007, but one was trash by 2010 even after spending $300 dollars on a repair job. six months later they told me the hard-drive was fried. I told the "Geek guy" he should have told me that before I wasted more money adding a Video Card …(muckin jerks!) So I'm typing this book on a used $89 Laptop, because I don't have much of anything that I used to have…such is life.

So I will just stick to asking the Laptop to type; I can listen to the message on the CD player later. So where was I…?

Oh yea! I picked up my CD of Sunday's message and headed into the sanctuary. I got the call reminding me to pick it up while I was as work; that was a pleasant surprise. When I saw the name "City Church" comes up on my cell phone, I thought,

"Who would be calling me from there; ain't nobody got my number?"

So when I answered and she mentioned the CD I said,

"Ohhh…ok, I'll see you at 7pm."

All the while knowing that was a "faith" statement cause I knew there wasn't hardly any gas in my car. And I wasn't even sure if I would make it to church.

So after I got off work, I made one stop. It didn't pan out; I was suppose to meet my cousin Viva to repair something for her, but she wasn't there. Then I was to head home (not my place). I needed to stop at the store and get a fruit, but I only had a dollar. So I settled for one banana. I went to a cashier named Moriah because it's always good to look in the face of a pretty girl than some guy. She had waited on me one time before late one night, but today she seemed to be on another planet. No smiles, no nothing; and the customer in front of me was no help. She was just going on & on about nothing, and it took forever to just hit the buttons on the debit machine. I was like,

"OH MY GOODNESS, could she please SHUT UP! MOVE ON! Or talk about something interesting...Lady... please!

And that's one of the reasons I love people; LIFE gives us all types. How could a Writer possible get bored and not have material to write about. Or not make you laugh, when there is so much material available. I told the cashier,

"Did you see her; she was taking forever telling the story…a word…per breath…while she fumbled trying find debit card, driver's license, and Winn-Dixie card? How long it takes to swipe ya card?... ½ a second? And did ya see the two packs of bread she left? She said she changed her mind; she didn't want the bread anymore. I thought, my goodness she should have done that 10 years ago before she reached the 500 lbs mark."

Of course I would never say any of this out loud…that would be mean. Plus, that's just not me. I just have the habit of observing people, making assessments, and seeing how close to the truth I am. And with the gift of discernment, sometimes the information can be right on. Then I'll just let the Holy Spirit confirm what's going on, and learn a few lessons for the day.

Well I left the store, headed to the house; laid down for a few minutes while I tried to listen to some study material by JOHN G. LAKE. He was an awesome "conduit" for GOD's word to help heal people in the early twenties. One testimony I found incredible was the story of how Mr. Lake prophesied the name & man that would take over the Ministry GOD gave him. This person that Mr Lake prophesied wasn't even born yet, and I thought that was pretty awesome. That man was named… BLAKE CURRY, and he would pick up where Mr Lake left off. If you ever get to read the story, you'll see that

Blake Curry is, and John G. Lake was… Pretty awesome Men of GOD!

After listening to the Pastor, and listening to the songs, I headed to my car. I saw a familiar face in the bookstore, so I darted in to ask a question. The young lady called me by name,

"hello SIR"

"Oh hi, can I ask you a question," I said.

I proceeded to ask about Sunday's service and one of the songs (I'm free) that was sung doing service. I also wanted to know if the church had a CD of it, or at least produced a video of it. Because the anointing that resonated during that performance was pretty palpable; I couldn't wait to see if I could get a copy. But the young lady told me that there was no such copy available, because it wasn't their song, and they didn't own the copyright.

As I exited the parking lot, I pondered this thought. I thought it amazing how many churches today try to lay claim to the Gospel. And how it's a common practice for Preachers, Teachers, and Evangelist all want to put a price on their material that they preached about the Gospel. GOD gives a Singer a song. And now he thinks he owns it. The Gospel (of JESUS CHRIST) belongs to GOD. He freely gave it to us, yet we have the audacity to want to be compensated for something that we can't even lay claim. I know these are "crazy words" in many Christian circles, but I just tell it how GOD gives it to me. No Man, No Church, No Religion… owns the Gospel! And yet, we act like we do.

I thought about the guy who may have written the song "I'm Free"; there sure isn't much freedom attached to using it.

In the course of our conversation, I was trying to find out who do I need to speak with about the footage from Sunday service of the song. I wanted to use the clip to make a video. She went on to add that they couldn't give it to me because they couldn't sell it; they don't own it. I thought,

"Who's talking about selling it…why don't ya just GIVE it away!"

At that point she told me that either way, the question or idea would have to be directed to the Pastor. I thanked her, and headed to my car; amazed at some of the responses I get from these "traditionalist". We want the move of GOD, but nobody wants to "bend"…bend the rules (even break some of them), bend on your knees, bend & bow to GOD's way of doing things, and not tradition. I like how Blake Curry once commented on Revival. He said,

"I'm not waiting or praying for a move of GOD…I AM A MOVE OF GOD!!

…and that summed it up for me.

Today also was the start of the 21day Fast that Pastor has proclaimed for the church. I had forgotten about it, but you can say I had already started and didn't even realize it. I had a breast yesterday (let me clarify…that was a chicken breast); then I ate the other ½ of it for breakfast (Umm that should count as I meal). Then I had a crab for lunch (took me about 45 minutes to eat it…I don't like food I got to fight with to eat…

...I'll eat a few boil shrimps(4 or 5); they gotta be big though. I don't care much for crawfish (too much trouble for so little reward). And I'll eat a nice crab every "blue moon". After that, I'm good when it comes to seafood.

"And yes, this boy is from Naw'awlins! and I can cook a mean pot of GUMBO!"

Well I made it to the house, and pull out the Laptop so I could get started writing. I didn't want to forget nuthin, so I just went straight to the room and started pecking away. Was hungry, but decided to wait after midnight. It's 2 am now, and I have to be to work for 7:30am. So I guess I betta either go to sleep, or get a snack and go to sleep; either way I gotta..."go ta sleep."

The church also is suppose to meet for Prayer for 7:00am. Well I got to be at work for 7:30am and I don't know how anybody can make it if they have to be to work for 8:00am; prayer meeting is over at 8:00. I think 6:00am would have been better. ..just a thought.

Well, after I told the Lord goodnight and, "See ya in church…"City Church"; I said thank YOU JESUS for keepin it REAL, Keepin ME real, and for BEING REAL in my LIFE.

CHAPTER 2… Sunday September 15, 2013….(I know it's late, but better late than not at all; enjoy!)

WOW!...what a Sunday Service! This particular Sunday there seem to have been a shift. I'll try to explain as I go (HOLY SPIRIT, please assist me; I cannot do it alone).

I wrote down the scriptures and notes from the service (pause)…

GOD just spoke via a loud thundering that just occurred outside; perfect timing and a perfect analogy.

As I was saying…

… I was lead to write the scriptures down. And, I felt the importance of writing them down this particular time.

I'm very tired right now, so I'll pick up tomorrow. I've been writing other projects since about 9:30pm; it is about 2:25am and I've been at it for almost 5 hours nonstop. I only type 45 to 50 words a minute, and at times I have a non-cooperative keyboard with non-compliant fingers that do there on thang at time. LORD willing, we'll pick up here tomorrow.

Buenos noches!...for now.

While I was yet on my knees praying, and even as I write now; the VOICE of GOD (Thunder) spoke very loud, and very clear. And all that I could say was YES LORD…thy will be done. I don't know what many hear when they hear thunder, or see when they see Lighting, but I HEAR the voice of GOD, and I SEE his MAJESTY & GLORY!

"…thank YOU LORD JESUS… HOLY SPIRIT… HEAVENLY FATHER for speaking to your Servant, and hearing your VOICE loud and clear, feeling your POWER, and possessing the righteous

FEAR of a Servant of GOD…down to my very Soul…AMEN."

…continuing from yesterday
Well it's about 8:15pm; it has been a long day. Got off work at about the usual time, but this time I was about to slap the hell out somebody. But I just made a phone call, and gonna handle it that way.

I'm amazed at how you cannot give everybody a title because it goes to their head, and they become another Hitler. I'm black, born & raised in New Orleans, speak Spanish, look good, very intelligent, and don't kiss no body's ass…black, white, or Spanish. I guess she thought I'm suppose to kiss hers, butt (excuse the pun) it ain't happening. ..

"Like I always say, when it comes to a 9-5

12 Months From Now/Book II

It's just a J. O. B. ya see

That's all it's ever gonna be to me;

It'll neva be more than that

Just as sho as my ass is black;

So don't trip, and get it twisted;

If they didn't appreciate ya work

You won't even miss it."

When I work at a job, I give the people I work for (and work with), their money's worth. Ask any place I worked, and anyone I've ever worked with.

This Spanish person I'm currently supervised by obviously has a "negro problem"; but I'm gonna get her together. She got one mo time to try and throw me "under the bus", and I'm gonna "call her out"...but I digress (again)...sorry. I'm supposed to stay focus.

Oh yea...the scriptures. I'm not sure if it was the first scripture Pastor mention, but it was the first one I wrote down. Matt 7:7-11 talks about "Asking"...and how GOD wants to give good gifts to HIS children when we ask. I went on to write down the other scriptures that Pastor mentioned, and being already familiar with them, I opened the Bible and started to read the first verse that caught my eye. It was the Book of II Kings 4 Chapter 10-38 verse; as I read, the tears began to just flow. Elisha (one of my favorite Prophets) and the Shunammite women is a great example of the power of GOD and the anointing given unto the "Man of GOD" to bless the women. She took care of the "Man of GOD" and she was blessed with a son (you know the scriptures). I've read it so very often, and it touches my very soul every time. Pastor talking about asking GOD, while GOD is talking about how HE so wants to give good gifts unto HIS children. So much was being revealed to me in that moment I felt like I would just scream.

Scream! thanking GOD for HIS goodness, HIS kindness, and HIS mercy, and HIS grace; Ohhhhh, how I have been blessed by HIS goodness, mercy, kindness, & grace. I'm forever thankful…in JESUS name…Amen.

And when they began to sing the song "I'm free", it was the perfect choice because truly I'm free, and want no part of religious, spiritual, emotional, mental, or physical bondage. And as I was sitting there, all I could think of was,

"Boy this footage would make a great video…"

"I wonder if they made a video of this song yet…?"

"Who do I need to talk to about doing a video with this footage; I can just see captives being set free!"

I sang the song to myself, all the way home because that's the kind of anointing I saw resting upon that performance while standing there…SOUL-4ever-set- free anointing.

As I'm trying to write, my fingers don't want to cooperate; I keep hitting the wrong keys. I'm so tired, I keep dozing off. And I've had to correct so many punctuation errors since being so tired; I might as well just stop and get ready for bed.

Today I was hoping to get a surprise phone call or something; maybe even a note attached to my windshield from an old friend. I guess it'll take a miracle to make any of that happen. In the meantime I'm also looking forward to a few million dollars to just pop-up from out of nowhere. It really doesn't matter to me the source of this blessing, I just know that I'm ready (been ready) to receive it…in JESUS name…Amen.

I ate my one meal a day about two hours ago after stopping by my "play sister" Angela. KT cooked, and the "dirty rice" was great. But then I could eat plain rice or with butter, all day long…I LOVE ME SOME RICE!

Dirty rice, shrimp fried rice, butter & rice, red beans & rice, gravy & rice, chicken soup & rice, gumbo w/rice, cabbage & rice, white beans & rice, chili & rice, pork & beans w/ground meat (my favorite thanks to my first wife) & rice, green beans & rice, and just plain RICE! Do you think I love rice? Ohhh yea…I LOVE ME SOME RICE!

I have the choice between jasmine rice, parboil rice, and regular rice. But if you ever bring me some "minute maid" crap, I'm gonna throw it back at cha!

This how I like my rice: cooked on the stove with an ½ inch of water above the rice line in the pot…started out with the fire high? Then turned to low with the lid placed on it after it starts to boil? Three minutes later, turn the fire off and leave the lid on while it continues to cook with no fire. If it is not prepared for me this way…keep it! …I don't want it. I do not like gummy rice.

Oh my LORD…Pastor has placed us on a 21day fast, and I guess that's why I'm sitting here writing about how much I love RICE. Well at least I'm not hungry. I ate yesterday at about lunchtime (a boil crab), and if I had anything else I don't remember…oh yea!...I had that one banana too. It was a small one. Other than that, I didn't eat again until about 9:30am this morning…I was starving! My co-worker (Alejandro) bought me a sausage biscuit &an egg sausage burrito (never had one). I don't eat that crap; eggs wrapped in a tortilla…only thing I want to eat wrap in a tortilla is meat, carne, beef…that's it! You can keep the "sucker food". These restaurants take crap, wrap it in something and call it a pretty name, and people break their necks to buy it; just give me some meat, and I'll be fine. I don't have an appetite for pork or catfish that much anymore; I guess with Wisdom, comes Wisdom? (LOL). I bet you thought I was gonna say…

(sorry, still didn't say it). The Bible says,

> "…You have what you say."

So I'll take the Wisdom, just keep the…

"AGE"…there I said it! Now chill; I ain't got no hang ups with getting older…just lookin old. (LOL).

Well, I need to go to sleep cause I'm tired. Tomorrow is Friday, and I think there is something at the church on Fridays but I really don't know. Don't know, and don't really know where to look. During the announcements segment, they show some kind of gathering or social scene for adults (18 yrs & older), but I'm really not interested in "meet & greet" right now. I'm past the dating scene, and have already been down the aisle twice…well actually never been down the aisle yet. Both were "Justice of the Peace" ceremonies; I wish they were both big church weddings, especially the last one, but I never had the pleasure or privilege. I could have had it with the 2nd wife, but she was always pregnant when we would plan the wedding (she wanted children so bad, till she just couldn't wait. Now I wish she would have waited like I asked her to; my children wouldn't be in the mess she have place them in with this sorry-ass nigga she with. Yes that's what he is…a sorry-ass nigga. I call it like I see it. And I don't mind "keeping it REAL!"

I thought both marriages would last forever...but they didn't.

But I learned that everybody don't love GOD, that says they love GOD (or that say they love YOU).

So when things changed, and the person you with, want to be with someone else?...let em!

LIFE goes on...and goes on with or without them. And if you choose to stay close to GOD, there will be many days they wish they never did what they did. Read ya Bible baby...it's in black & white (red when JESUS spoke) letters.

...So I'm cool...and it's gonna be pretty cool where I'm headed when I leave here(earth).

SLEEP is really calling me now. So until Sunday Service (or Friday if I find out something is going on there on Fridays), be cool, be bless, and T.G.B.T.G!

I'm SIR…theSOULman. Like I say in all my productions when I close,

"If I don't see YOU here, I HOPE I see YOU there"…(as I point to the Heavens)

10:53pm/9-19-13

SUNDAY SERVICE Sept. 22,2013

(hope & praying…no…I speak miracles.
Come forth!...in JESUS name)

It's about 11pm now, and it's still Thursday night (an hour before midnight).

I thought I would go ahead and type my title now, so I can be ready to type my entry in after church on Sunday. I was about to say I'm expecting a miracle but I change that to,

"I AM a MIRACLE, AND I SPEAK MIRACLES IN TO EXISTENCE."

MIRACLES COME FORTH…IN THE NAME OF JESUS!. YOU ARE COMMANDED BY THE BLOOD OF CHRIST, AND BY THE WORD OF THE LIVING GOD! COME FORTH…NOW…IN JESUS NAME…

…AMEN…AMEN…and…AMEN!"

Every day we must allow ourselves to be used by GOD, lead by the HOLY SPIRIT, and come before GOD in the name of JESUS. So that prayers will be answered, "captives" will be set free, and the WORD of GOD becomes real in our lives, and seen with our own eyes. It's "time-out" for playing, and it's time-out for "playing church."

"JESUS is on HIS way, and if the CHURCH don't act like it, how is the World gonna know!"

...until we meet again on Sunday.

Friday morn...6:43am

As you can see from the above entry that Sunday came early for me. The Spirit of the LORD awakens me, and I looked at my cell phone and it read 4:44am. I've grown accustom to being awaken by the LORD, and I know that a message is to be delivered to me, and a very important one (well they all are important). As usual I awaken, struggled with a flesh matter (satan always trying to put his 1cent in), but didn't allow myself to be condemned. Dealt with the flesh matter, moved on, prayed to the LORD JESUS, and got ready for the message.

As to be expected, the LORD delivered; and it was a powerful one. If anybody (with any sense) truly seeks the TRUTH and wants to HEAR the TRUTH, then I encourage you to go to "YouTube" and go to "Sword of the Spirit" channel or just click on "Mike Hoggard"…you will be Amazed by his "the missing King James Bible" piece he did. Pretty awesome, and it will be hard for a lot of "religious" people to stomach. If ya stuck on your religion, you gonna get ya feelings hurt watching this…and it don't matter what religion you stuck on (mormon, catholic, Baptist, Jehovah witness, etc.) This information is gonna "shatter your world".

Well it's almost 7am. I got to get ready for work and be there in 30 minutes...T.G.B.T.G!!! And if you read anything I've ever written, you know what that means already. Be bless...in JESUS name...Amen!

Sunday 11:00 am Service
... don't know why I thought Service started for 10:30 am

Well, either my clock in the car was wrong, or I just was out of sync with the day's activities. I got to church early, but didn't realize I was early until I walked in. People were standing in the front getting prayed for, and I thought I'd missed something. Then when one of the usher asked if I was there for the 9 o'clock service or the 11o'clock, I realize then the crowd I was looking at was about to go home.

I took my usual sit in the rear, and waited till Pastor dismissed the congregation. After the service was over, there was about 15 minutes of socializing amongst the members before the next service began. Of course there was no socializing for me because I still don't really know anyone. I know the Pastor and the Bishop's name (McManus), that's about it. If anyone else mentioned or told me their name, I've forgotten it. Life for me right now is so crazy and senseless outside church, till I can't do much concentrating on what's going on inside church. I used to feel so at home no matter what church I entered, now I feel like a fish out of water.

When I first started attending the "Potter's House", we were a loving & happy family. Now I don't even want to talk about the "mess" of my life now. It's like what all those years at the "Potter's House" was for? Satan was successful at tearing down & destroying everything I worked for since recovering from Katrina. I was already recovering from the first divorce, and was homeless & living in my office where I had my recording studio. Had just started back working, and getting on my feet; then "BAM!" Katrina hits. "And the rest is history," as they say.

Church was very good, and it was so good I said I would remember to suggest to everyone to be sure to get copy of today's message. There were so many things pointed out in the message that I was already thinking about while in the car on the way to church. Of course I can't even think of any of it right now. I just have so much on my mind. So many questions I'm pondering trying to understand the state of my Life. Too much to even mention here; all I know…Life Stinks!

I work; I don't have no money. Even on the job I have to fight for my rightful place. Don't know where my children are. My older kids all need money too, and I can't send them anything because I'm being "robbed" by a devil inspired system. Haven't heard a word from Tiffany; sent two letters (explaining myself clearly) and invited her (and a friend if there is one) to the Movie premiere while also paying(for the tickets myself…no response. Even invited the girl at the door who I gave the letters to give to her (Teirra…I think that's how it's spelled); no response from her either. Got tickets to "Arsenio"; probably won't make it. Still staying at my "play sister"; still no house of my own eventhough I've own at least 10 properties (4 homes, 6 rentals) at least 30 cars, furnishings, etc. All gone; lost, foreclosed, repossessed. …thanks to "loose" wives who couldn't keep their panties up and their skirts down. Again…that's another story.

So when I think about all of this, me spending my whole life striving to do right, be a faithful husband and great father/Dad to my children I ask,

"What was the point?"

"Do nice guys really finish last?"

Yea I'll get my reward one day when I get to Heaven, but "What about now?"

So many Lies are being preached in so many churches; so many untruths are being taught; and so many prayers are not being answered.

"Why?"

Because so many are being deceived; so many think they are saved and are not; and so many churches are ignoring "GOD's voice" and are listening to their own. "Own agenda" is one of the most dangerous things to have when it comes to Ministry; I learned this many years ago during my first period of Ministry training. I've watched lives lost, and lives destroyed because of people in the Ministry being mislead, and misleading others. Satan is a Deceiver, and he is very good at deceiving many. But if and when one is truly submissive to the "Spirit of the LORD", have the Word abiding in you while you abide in CHRIST, you don't have to ever be deceived.

Well, just get the message Pastor preached on this Sunday service. It speaks for itself, and says what I just can't put into words right now. Too much I just don't understand concerning my Life, and it just has me down. I just want to understand the "whys" of how I got here. Cause if where I'm at right now today is solely because of my own doing, thinking, or believing, then that's very disappointing. Because to do wrong, while believing you are doing what's right, is a very sad state to be in. The things I've had to suffer, I wouldn't wish it on my worst enemy…not even on "mad day". The Bible says,

"There is a way that seemeth right unto man, but whose path leadeth unto destruction."

...I don't want to be that kind of person.

I'm trying to remember other highlights of this day's service, but things are just a fog. Oh yea, there was a little gathering for the new members after service. I stopped and grab a snack. I spoke with a Pastor Benson; he sung the "Our Father" prayer during service and he has an absolutely marvelous voice. I believe he has, or does sing professionally.

One more thing I want to note. I was thinking about the "first time visitors" when they come to City Church. I think they should really do interviews with all of them after service to get their views on the experience. I can tell from the look & body language of some that they are pretty "blown away." I'm sure many (especially the college crowd) are thinking,

"Is this really church? I don't remember church being this LIVE when I was little…they are having too much fun…it's like a concert."

I'm sure the older crowd has a totally different response, but either way I think it would be interesting to get "first time visitors" feedback. Even though I do media, and I'm a veteran when it comes to church & ministry, I still was in awe of the whole experience. This is the "media generation" and you have to use media to reach them when it comes to Ministry." You have to speak the language this generation understands…and then you'll have a chance to reach them for CHRIST.

Now don't get me wrong; satan is also using media to reach this generation. One of the main ways right now is the cell phone. Too much focus and attention is given to cell phones and all the activities that it affords you, besides talking. When I see children (especially adults) in church playing games with their cell phones and IPads, I just cringe. They don't know how deadly of a game they are really playing. In church, your focus should be on GOD the Father, CHRIST the Son, and the Holy Spirit. And whoever is bringing the message or speaking while in church, that's where your attention should be.

One day while sitting in church when I was attending the Potter's House of Dallas, the "Spirit of the LORD" spoke very clear to me while watching this teenager playing games on his phone.

"Because of those, many will go to Hell."

I was so grieved in my spirit; then I thought about how it was a cell phone that got my wife in trouble and help lured her away from all that she knew to be good. It was with that thing, she began to send naked pics to complete strangers while I was working nights. And as I thought about all of this, I knew, many are sitting right in church today clueless to the danger they place themselves in, by their activities, their lifestyle, their friends, and what they believe to be "truth." All glitter ain't gold, and all knowledge ain't TRUTH".

So when I see adults & children so in grossed by these little gadgets that seem to have taken over their lives, I just cringe…because nothing I say could ever convince them otherwise. For "…the god of this world has their eyes/minds blinded…".

Well I guess I should try to sleep now. It's about 11:30pm, and I need to work in the morning. Tomorrow is Wednesday (Bible study), and I needed to get this done so that I could make room for Wednesday night entry. I haven't been able to attend morning prayer since I have to be to work for 7:30am but all is well; I pray at home. When I go to bed, and when I get up; and the most amazing thing is that sometimes the little things are what we neglect that can make all the difference in the world. I pray all the time (I talk to GOD all day long sending up prayers constantly, asking questions, just having conversation), but somehow I had let the "Our Father" prayer slip by me. I didn't realize that I was neglecting this prayer, and also neglecting to get on my knees at night and pray. And this is how the enemy gets us, forgetting to do the little things. Well I'm back on my knees, (morning & night-time), and I always bless my food (that I don't forget)…

(pause)

…Computer crashed again; this makes at least the 10th time tonight, and I'm getting so frustrated. I was making a very good point, and now it's gone. I'll try and see if I can remember what I wrote. Here goes…

(stupid muckin jerk…I was about to sign off and go to bed)…What was I saying?

Let's see, oh yea!

I was talking about praying for your food and how important it was. Then I mentioned how I had a video on my "You tube" channel, and how it turned out great (@sirfinis), but it didn't get as many hits as the one about my wife when I recorded her on the cell phone yelling & cussing me out. Everybody loved that one, but I talked about how I deleted it because I didn't want her to be continually seen in a negative light. Yes she was just like a demon possessed person(NO...she was one), but I felt maybe someday she would find GOD again...hopefully.

I talked about all those things and was about to sign off when the computer crashed. I try to save my info every few seconds (this doesn't have auto save like the newer version), but sometimes I be making a point, and I forget to save after a few minutes.

So what I originally wrote is forever in cyberspace; I'm just thankful that it saved what it did. I know it's not a 2013 Laptop, but it's getting the job done…

…thank YOU LORD JESUS! For everything!

Where would I be without YOU!

..Huh?

…I'd be done lost my mind!!!

Simple as that…(Thank YOU LORD for saving ME!)

…in JESUS name,…Amen.

Wednesday night Biblestudy

...not just another Wednesday night;

(I'm going to go and say my prayers now and go to sleep. LORD willing, I'll be back here on tomorrow (well today; it's 12:27am) Good nite!...(press save button)

Well I didn't make it back; it's actually 5:55 in the morning. I was awaken a few minutes ago as I was having some crazy dream…didn't quite get it. So I decided to stay up and make this entry.

The day (Thursday) was going ok until 3:00 pm. I got a call from my ex-mother-in-law who hasn't spoken to me in almost two years. She told me CPS got my kids and my ex-wife is locked up in psych ward trying to kill herself over a sorry-ass nigga. My response was simple,

"Why the hell they call you and not me?"

She was calling me to ask if I could take her to get my kids cause she didn't have a way (or any money). I told her I can go get my own kids; and I don't need an escort.

If it wasn't for her mother, my children's mother wouldn't be in the mess she is in now (yea… I know satan is at fault too). But if CHRIST is in your life, and in your heart, satan cannot succeed at deceiving you.

You see, my ex wife is my ex wife because of her mother. It was her mother who told her she need a younger man. But I don't fault her mother totally; the whole family is messed up. Plus, no one can talk you in to doing something that is not already set in your mind/heart to do.

So I told her mom I would call her back after I try to reach CPS. After calling around, I got the info I needed, said a prayer, and put the matter in the hands of GOD.

Well Bible study was great. Pastor talked about Joseph…

…(wow it was so fresh in my mind…now it's gone. I guess it's the trauma of the previous day (its Friday morning now). I guess I'll go pray some more).

Well after the service, I attended the "meet & greet belong" meeting afterwards. Didn't get out till about 10:30pm. After watching the video, and learning of the history of the ministry, some of its members, and the McManus family, I was truly impressed. Not that I wasn't before (GOD wouldn't just send me anywhere). But the longevity of the members & the ministry (without the drama) was very impressive to me. I felt so humbled; with my just coming in the door, just sweeping the floor in the sanctuary would be an honor position for me as far as I was concern. I thought about the ordination service, and thought of the gentleman (sorry, but I'm still learning names) who came to church when he was six (we talked at the meeting for a bit) and he is now 26 or 27 yrs old…that in itself is a great honor. And to be under one Ministry & one Minister for so long, and have such a close relationship with him, I bow down to the dedication, commitment, &loyalty that they have shown the "Man of GOD." And from what the Holy Spirit has taught me over the years, it says a lot about him. His integrity and commitment to GOD and the calling on his LIFE has obviously not been taken lightly, or for granted. I bow & honor the "spirit of dedication & commitment" that GOD has placed on this Ministry, and the lives of the Men and Women of GOD he has placed in the midst.

Well with church being so long and so good, I thought I would have so much more to write. But I guess sometimes the few the words, says it best. After the meeting, I can now say,

"I now "belong" and feel I'm a part of City Church."

And no longer feel like a stranger. I just wished I had known, and been a part of this Ministry before satan stepped in and deceived my wife. Who then lost her morals, while I nearly lost my mind after she was lured out into that world of the "broad & wide" that leadeth to destruction. There was just "no help" from where I was attending…none…nada!

I guess that's one of the drawbacks of mega churches; you get lost in the crowd, and become just another number. I prayed & fasted, and did all I could to try and fight that demon & spirit of "Lies & Lust". But it was just too big and too strong for me to fight alone. GOD says one will send a thousand a flight, and two ten thousand. Soooo, I guess it was more than a legion of demons, cause I was not able to save the wife I married…from her own self. Or from the lust that she had in her heart.

And I shed tears even now as I think about it because I know she didn't have to go through that unnecessary hell. Even though she was, and is the wife that I prayed to have, and that GOD gave me, it didn't make her exempt from an attack of the enemy (many would think so though).

But it doesn't. So to all the married couples in the world; this is a major lesson for your "GOD appointed relationship". Don't underestimate the power of deception; and don't think because she loves you now, she can't hate you later.

…been there;

done that!

My wife still loves me; but the power of deception has lead her down that path of unrighteousness. And since we were no longer "two that walked together" and was not in agreement (she wanted the world; I knew enough to stay with GOD), our parting ways was inevitable. I've prayed for her so many times, and have seen a many answer prayers (barren wombs bringing forth a child to cancer being stopped in its tracks) but I've learn you have to want what GOD wants for your life…even if it's the "crumbs from the Master's table". But she no longer wanted what GOD had planned for her Life; she liked what satan had to offer her and wouldn't listen to nothing I had to say. Even after GOD warned her many times in a dream. So like the Word says,

"…GOD will allow satan to take your life, to save your soul…".

And experience has taught me that many have left this world before their time (by the millions) because the path they were walking on was not the path GOD chose for their Life.

"I've chosen LIFE, and also chosen it for all my children…and LIFE more abundantly that I have chosen, will be the LIFE that I will have for me and my children! And if there is ever a wife again sometime in the near future, she will soon learn,

"I change for NO ONE, and will not serve no other GOD but the Almighty GOD that made Heaven & Earth, and all within it.

Satan has nothing to offer my family lineage, and I DECLARE he is not welcome, allowed, or will have any part in the Life of myself or, the Life of my children. As for a wife; no more having to teach them about GOD…they got to know HIM already for themselves! If anything, they need to "come correct" and be able to share with me some of the revelations (straight from the throne of GOD) that

GOD has given them. And if they are truly "sold out" for CHRIST, their piece of the puzzle that GOD has given them, will fit perfectly with the piece of the puzzle that GOD has already given me…T.G.B.T.G!

Be bless, and I'll see ya soon. And like I always say in closing,

"If I don't see YOU here, I hope I see YOU there!"

Sunday 11am Service September 29th …my three (3) DAUGHTER'S very 1ST City church Experience

Payday came Friday, and as usual the 50 to 55% that the state was illegally taking out of my check was not at my disposal yet again. So with the $270.00 that was left over, I made plans to see if I would be going to Texas for my final furniture move. It had already been almost 60 days since my latest home was foreclosed on, so I knew I didn't have much time left to remove any remaining items out of the home. The trip had been planned for weeks, but was postponed several times due to the lack of finances. But since Thursday of September 26, 2013, this trip wasn't going to be postponed.

You see, by the end of the day, I had received a call from my ex-mother-in-law. And since receiving this call, my three daughters that I love and had been missing dearly, was now with me in my custody here in New Orleans.

And their lovely mother? Well I soon found out their "hard-head-don't-want-to-listen-to-no-one including-GOD" mother was now somewhere in Dallas at Parkland hospital on the psych ward. It seems that while during a routine visit, she struck the boyfriend in the head with the cell phone right in front of the CPS worker. After the violent display, the CPS worker grabbed the kids, placed them in the car, and called for back-up.

When she flipped out in front the CPS worker, the LIE her and her "crooked-no-good- slime" of a lawyer told in court to get custody of the children, was now null & void. All his Lies and "legal bag of tricks" couldn't save her now. And you know what's so funny and amazing? The CPS worker's name that filed the report and requested that the kids be removed from her care, was the same as mine: BREWER (no relation). I thought, "WOW! GOD really has a sense of humor.

Well after receiving this call from the ex mother-in-law to take her to Texas, I thought,

"Wow, what a nerve of some people."

Weeks earlier when her daughter (my ex) was here in New Orleans escaping a domestic violence situation with the same guy, and a jail promise from the Fort Worth Police, she sat on her porch and acted like she never knew me. You would have thought I was a dead dog from hell. She must have been draggin for me and talking about me like a dog for the past 18 months. She sat on that porch and never said a word to me the two times I visited to see my kids while they were here with their mother. Now she was calling me telling me that CPS called her and said,

"Come get the children."

She had no car, couldn't drive, and wasn't that thrill about the responsibility of having to care for 3 grandchildren, so I guess she swallowed her pride, and called her ex son-in-law whose marriage she personally help to destroy. She was the one who told my wife,

"You need to go get you a younger man."

 So I really didn't have much to say to her. But not being one to whole grudges, I acted just like nothing ever happened, and spoke with her very politely to get the matter concerning my children, addressed.

Even after meeting my wife, I knew that the whole family had problems, just from the way my wife used to talk to her mother and they cuss each other out like they were friends, and not mother & daughter. It was the craziest thang I'd ever seen in my life. So I thought,

"This got to be why GOD brought us together? Whatever we each needed, we both would fulfill those needs".

And there definitely was some "light at the end of the tunnel" since she had become my wife. But I guess you got to want what GOD wants for you. But how can that happen when you don't even know, that you don't KNOW GOD. You may know of HIM, but don't have a clue about… WHO GOD is.

Well after I realize who it was that was calling me, and that my children may have been in danger, the first question I asked was,

"Why in the hell they didn't call me! I'm the Father!

And after I cooled down and got myself together, I quietly asked what was going on. After many years in the Ministry, I've learned a many things. One of them is this,

"As a True Born Again Believer who Trust & Believe in the True & Almighty Living GOD, I've learned to PRAY first. No longer do I break my neck trying to run to fix something I can't fix; or run to the hospital worrying about the outcome." If you are a True Believer, you're going to PRAY first, and then decide on your next move. If the Holy Spirit say go, then you move.

So after she told me a little about what had happen, I then told her I will be working till Friday evening, will get off at 5pm, and then make plans to go get my children. As I was making these plans, I thought to myself as my blood began to boil once more,

"I definitely didn't need an escort to go pick up my own kids (from Texas)." "And I definitely did not appreciate not being called first."

The "Word of GOD" says,

"If GOD is for YOU, who can be against you?"

And thanks to my standing on this WORD, I now have my three daughters here in New Orleans with me. And at the moment, I'm making every effort to do away with the "spiritually illegal" access to my finances/theft/robbery that the state of Texas is committing against me and my children.

Many people think "child support" is some kind of blessing, and has GOD's approval. But this method of degrading fathers and robbing them by an unlawful law, is straight from the "pits of Hell". It is another one of satan's clever little ways to destroy & attack the family. Undermine, belittle, destroy the image, rob, imprison, and remove the "head", and you got the whole family. So many are going to be in for the shock of their lives when they stand before GOD; thinking they were such a "good person" doing what they were doing. But all the while they were punching satan's Time clock and getting his work done. If any law, practice, or entity/agency works to place the image of a father in a negative light, or remove him out of his rightful GOD-given place as head of the family, it's the work of the devil. The government had "good intentions" when they first started these programs to assist Women & children, but these programs have evolved to do one thing and one thing only:

"Do the Father's job, and take his place as head, and provider of the family."

Now unfortunately, the government has deemed family as two women & child/children; two men & child/children; or a single mother & child/children, and only recently a father and a child/children. In the past, the system would almost never give or allow the father to have his children.

The LORD has only one description of Family, and it embraces the natural "laws of GOD" that HE has set for man. But like so many "good intentions" of man, satan has as usual infiltrated these "good intentions" and is now guiding the hands of his "unsuspecting employees" to get his work done. Which ultimately is: to destroy

Family. The Word says, "…satan has come to steal, kill, and destroy." Look around…he is definitely getting his work done with the help of a lot of non/fake Christians. If you are listening or reading this passage, I hope you are not one of them.

Well I left Friday at 3am (after getting a little nap) to drive to Texas to get my children, and made it back by Sunday morning to make it to City church. The first thing I wanted my daughters to do when they got home here in New Orleans was to be found in the House of the LORD. And since I was now attending City Church, I couldn't wait for them to have the "City Church" experience.

We arrived in New Orleans about 6am after driving all night. I called my sister who lives in the east and asked her if it would be ok if we paused there and I take a nap before getting ready for church, and of course she was ok with it. So after arriving at her house, I tried to sleep for a few minutes, but it was not successful. My girls slept quietly throughout the road trip and, now they were wide awake and excited to be home with Daddy. So lacking any proper sleep myself, I just combed their hair, got them dressed and ready for church.

I opt to attend the 11am service instead of the 9 o'clock just in case sleep came over me in the preceding hour. At least while still at my sister's house I could dozed off for a few minutes and it would be ok. As tired as I was, dozing off in church might cause a stir. Because when I'm very tired, I'm told that I snore…frankly I don't believe a word of it. My ex wives have said a lot of things about me that weren't true. This could be just another fabrication…

…ok, maybe I snore just a little bit ("tell the truth; shame the devil").

Well we arrived at church on time, and of course my girls were so excited. When "praise & worship" started, they were dancing in the aisle. I don't know if they were just excited about being in church (since they were raised going to church & loved to go), or just excited about being with their Daddy. They had been away from me for months, thanks to a flawed court system, bias judge, and corrupt lawyer with the laughable Law firm name of "minister of justice". And who also profess to hold a position in his church as a Minister. But thanks to an "Almighty GOD" who says, "…the truth will set you free", my daughters were now free from the Lies of a very flawed system that is supposed to be designed to protect children. Well I can speak from experience, and both times it has not protected my children from an adulterous mother who wanted welfare & the streets. Instead of a loving and faithful husband, who fathered their children. Many think "the grass is greener on the other side", and many some find out that it's just another LIE of satan. And the same government system that they depend on, and helps them to defy the "principles & laws of GOD" by making them think they are the "head" and they don't need a man. Is the same "government system" that is failing even now, and will answer to GOD for creating a false sense of hope in the lives of so many lost Souls. Who look and depend on the government, and never even acknowledge that GOD even exists.

October 2, 2013…Wednesday Bible study

(no entry)

October 6, 2013…Sunday 11am Service

(no entry)

October 9, 2013…Wednesday night Belong Service

(no entry)

October 11, 2013/Friday Night…start of the "2013 Power Conference"

Well I planned on taking my 3 daughters with me to the stage play, but to my surprise, my Sisters had other plans for them.

"Ok, big brother; the girls are having a "girls sleep-over" so you just gonna have to find something else to do for the weekend."

"Umm, jayla & janiyah say they don't want to stay so…"

"Well they are staying. We need to bond with our nieces since they haven't been around us."

As she pried my youngest daughter from my arms as she screamed for her daddy, I just accepted their fate…they were in "good hands."

I got to the sanctuary at about 7:37pm, and felt bad that I was running so late. The crowd was not as big as I expected, and I was a bit disappointed. By the time the stage play was over, there was many that came to mind that I felt should have been there. So many that crossed my mind; my children's mother was definitely one of them.

I left the church by 9:37, and it was quite interesting. I just wished it was the production that GOD had given me for the past 18 years. I'd been working so hard over the years I've written several plays, several songs, and many books. But I'm still waiting for "my turn"; when GOD says,

"NOW!"

And then the world will see what GOD has called me to do as I help usher in the:

"2ND COMING of CHRIST!"

Many don't know it, but WE ARE the generation that WILL see the 2nd Coming of JESUS CHRIST. And I'm amazed at the many churches that don't even have a clue. They have a whole different agenda, and unfortunately that agenda does not agree with the agenda of GOD.

October 13, 2013…Sunday 11am Service

Wow! …THE LIGHT SHOW WAS INCREDIDBLY AWESOME! While I was witnessing such an incredible display of talent, I felt bad that I put my kids in children church. They needed to witness this event as well, and I so wanted to go and pull them out of children's church, and seat them with me. There was one song that was sung that was great. It was Amazing Grace; it and the Light show brought tears to my eyes. I felt like the whole world should have been there, and witness the event.

October 15& 16, 2013…my 2nd eldest daughter 6th Birthday

Well the day didn't go as planned. Her Mother never sent any money for her gift, but to my surprise, her Teety Angela (my play sister) gave me her debit card to get her gift. All she wanted was an "Easy Bake Oven" for her birthday, and given a $60 budget by her "teety", that's what we purchased…and she was so very happy.

We didn't make it to church Wednesday night, the 16th because I still owed the $50 for the tickets to the Power Conference. I gave away the tickets instead of selling them for the Power Conference that the church had over the weekend, because I wanted to bless a few people. And if they didn't have the money, they could still get to attend a great event. I didn't have the money to spare, but I gave the tickets away still. I figure the Lord will bless, for being a blessing to others. So I guess I'll wait until I get paid to turn in the rest money. I just get tired of making excuses for not having any money, and tired of still being robbed by the state of Texas. Even though I've had my children for almost a month now, they are still "rippin me off" every week. They are full of excuses about not stopping the "child support" payments; and they are doing it illegally. But GOD doesn't sleep; every thief will have his day in "GOD's court". And by "what measure they have measure; it will be measured unto them…".

Later on m sister bought my daughter a nail set, and of course she was very excited about that gift as well. She painted her fingers & toes, her sister's finger & toes, and her cousin Jasmine's who shares her name, fingers & toes. It was a very Happy Birthday after all, and I was thankful to GOD for making a way.

I later checked my phone messages after discovering that it was off, and heard my children's mother's "nice" little message. I was wondering why I hadn't heard from her, and the phone being off clearly explained her not calling.

" I don't know why you not answering yo phone! I can't even call and wish my daughter a Happy Birthday…"

Well I feel like she should have been wherever her daughter was, instead of chasing that man she's committing adultery/fornication with…but I digress.

The following day was her mother's birthday, and after scraping up $10, I paid the phone bill, and the kids were able to call her and wish her a happy birthday. She told me that she no longer celebrated her birthday and I thought, "How sad". She has allowed another person to change her so much from her real self that she no longer even celebrates herself. Sin will make you do a lot of crazy things; even call wrong right, and right wrong. And that's all the results of being spiritually blind, carnal mind, and on your way to Hell.

Well I later wrote a piece concerning our little conversation, and just tucked it away with so many other pieces I've written prompt by incidents. Like so many, one day they'll all be read by the masses; that is if JESUS doesn't come back first.

October 17, Wednesday Bible Study

Well another Wednesday has passed, and I still haven't made it to church. I know in some circles & "belief systems" that would be like a major crime against your home church…to be a member, and just skip service. Well, I've freed myself from many religious beliefs & bondages long ago. We are supposed to attend church just like we should attend school. Both places we will learn the things that we need to know to be an asset in Life. But like school, if you miss a few days, it's not the end of the world, it's not gonna kill ya, and it won't send you to Hell (no matter what some religious preachers say).

 While in school, I never cut class, or played hooky; I never saw the point in any of it. Days I didn't feel like going (there weren't many) I just stayed home in my bed, helped my mother around the house, or just stayed inside. Education is very important to me, but since getting older, I've learned that a lot of what is being called education is not based on facts. There are a lot LIES flowing around out there being taught to our children, and the biggest one is trying to separate them from the knowledge of GOD. I have taught myself much of what I know (with much help from the Holy Spirit), and I credit no college degree for my intelligence. If degrees truly determined ones intelligence, we wouldn't have to pay so much to get them.

There are so many various forms of intelligence, till I'm left speechless by some examples. Like "Savants", Autistic kids, and true geniuses with incredible IQ's. And we must not forget the Animal World; there is so much intelligence in this realm that we haven't even begun to scratch the surface of this diverse form of GOD's creation.

When I get some money, I'll make it to church, and to Wednesday night Bible; but until then, I ain't trippin. I know how & when to Pray (everyday all day) and I know how to study my Word, and Minister to others as the Spirit of GOD leads. When I miss church, I don't like it but I ain't going to Hell. If anyone says I am, then tell them, "that's just another set of "bracelets& necklaces" religious folks trying to make you wear. I prefer chains of gold & silver; no longer care for "chains of bondage".

October 21, 2013 Sunday

Missed church; too embarrassed to pull up on that church parking lot with my car looking the way it was. Look like some giant took a bite out the back and ate the bumper. I even had to post something on face book…of course a few got quite a laugh out of it.

Face book (SirDemilo)

October 24, 2013..Wednesday night Bible study

Still no church, and still no bumper. I have to wait till I get paid, and even then I may not have enough to fix it. Well some might ask, "Are you paying your tithes?" My response would simple be…"NO"…I can't. If I make a few hundred dollars a week, and half is illegally being taken out, then the "tithe on the gross" belief goes out the window. And since all that is left is not even enough to pay the Day Care Provider who takes care of my daughter 5 days a week that blows the "first fruit" belief out the water. So anyway you look at my situation, as long as I'm being robbed by the State of Texas for "child support" that I should have never even been paying, tithing at the moment is not even possible. And I challenge anyone concerning my situation; cause I might not be seeing something that is very clear to someone else. Plus, I'm always open to dispelling LIES & untruths that are being passed off as "the Law of GOD". As long as the Spirit of GOD is doing the revealing, and not satan…you have my undivided attention. So to my constituents, and fellow Ministry people, here's the challenge:

$600 a week

$100 goes to Uncle Sam leaving $500

$260 being stolen by Texas leaving $240

$145 w/discount paid to Day Care Provider leaving $90

…what do I pay for tithes? $60 or $9; and I must have $45 to get kids & self back and forth to work and their school. What's your answer?

Hit me up on my Ministry Facebook page (Jammin4JesusProductions or email me at sirdemilo@yahoo.com)…I'm looking forward to all the responses

October 27, 2013…Sunday Service; honoring a commitment to visit Sister's church called Abundant Life on Hayne Blvd in "the East"

Well I was trying to make excuses for not going to church again, and while I was talking to my daughter (who is very keen & observant to certain things) and who just made 6 yrs old, she settled it for me. She was asking questions (like she normally do) and when I said I wasn't going to church she said,

"But Dad, you gotta go".

She said it with so much conviction, it was settled. She was right; I/we had to go. My kids always love going to church, and I hate that their mother wasn't taking them the months they have been with her. But I guess my wife couldn't face the reality in

'GOD's house" that she was living in sin, being rebellious, fornicating, committing adultery, lying to herself, others, and GOD and just down right "riding around Dirty".

So I decided that we would be going to church; then the phone rang. It was my Sister Mildred reminding me that I had a previous obligation to attend her church this coming Sunday to watch their dance group perform. Since I made the commitment, I was destine to be there.

The service was great; we rode over with my other Sister Lyn in her car. Her fiancée Donald drove; well I believe they are planning on getting married. I don't know how long they have known each other, but I have two Sister's now divorced due to infidelity, that are now with someone new, and they seem to be getting along very well. My other Sister Cyn has even bought a house with her new mate. I understand their marriage date is already set. The Sister who I was going to see perform with her dance group just celebrated 20 something years of marriage, and I'm so proud of her and her husband Greg. She told me the story how Mama told her to marry him, and at the time she wasn't even thinking about no marriage. She was still "fotting around" with her older children's father Eddie. Mama warned her about him, and Mama was so right. I was told he is currently in jail for something serious.

My other Sister Vyn husband died quite a few years ago; it was so very sad. He was very good to her, and loved the ground she walked on. Too bad they never had any kids together; I didn't know he was as sick as he was. I got a chance to film some of his funeral service, and it was quite a sight to see. When a "good man" leaves this world, I think even the angels in Heaven cry. Even though he was a New Orleans Police (and some have colorful reputation/straddling the fence between darkness & light) Regis was "a good man"; and he loved my Sister Vyn.

Well since we were only a few blocks from my own church, I wanted to go there as well, but my sister had other plans. We were riding with them, so we went where they went that day. I'll see if I can invite the whole family one Sunday, if they can see pulling themselves away from their own church for a minute…we'll see.

In the meantime, we made it back to Waggaman safely (thank GOD), and I got the girls to change their dresses and get in their play clothes, while I worked on my computer finishing up yet another book. This newest book is called "Stuck on Stupid" and it's a children's book. Sort of based on some unprompted conversations I've had with my daughter from the time that her mother left to be with her "rapper/boo" to now. It's a very interesting perspective for a children's book, but I feel it was the leading of the Holy Spirit. So no matter how far-fetched it may be or sound, I just do what I'm lead to do.

As far as the guy she is with now, they both have since regretted the "choices" they have made. All his furniture and car is tore up as well as the old apartment; they even were evicted from the one place. I've spoken with him on one occasion when I was lead to do so….no beef. Just man to whoremonger; ain't nothing for him and I to beef about anymore. She was married, he knew it, and she told a million LIES to get where she's at. Now he has suffered, and so has she, and they both will continue to have problems. Saying "I DO" to your husband means "You don't" to everybody else. And no matter who you are, or who you think you are, "lust" will never be LOVE in the eyes of GOD. I think it's a better legacy to give to your children the fact that they come from a "LOVE union" and not a sinful, adulterous one. I want nothing but the best for my children…that's why I married their mother, instead of making a whore out of her, like so many men do, and women allow them to do so (if you can't say Amen…say ouch!).

Riding with my Sister to church was her idea and it was ok, because it saved me from having to use my little gas in my car. Church Service was great, and the Pastor preached a good message. He preached about developing good relationships, and spoke about the Prophet Samuel (one of my favorites) and King David when he sent for provisions from Nebal & his wife Abigail..I love the story myself.

After service, I got to say hello to the "First Lady" and of course she was surprised to see me, and to see my three beautiful daughters. We chatted a few seconds, I gave her a nice hug as I said goodbye, and looked forward to seeing her when I finally put on a production of our own….JAMMIN4JESUS that is. She didn't know I had a production in the works. Well I do, and one of them is going to include the dance team that my sister is in, that I just witness. Because we all "Need a little JESUS".

October 30, 2013…Wednesday Night Bible Study

I really can't recall at the moment since it's almost a week later that I'm writing this, of why I didn't make it to Bible Study. I know part of it was my not having any money, and I was still needing to pay the remaining $50 dollars for the tickets that I was suppose to sell. I didn't sell them though; all of them were given away as a gift. Four were given to friends; four to strangers/someone I was hoping to see; and the remaining two I use for myself and my three daughters. So even though I was not in position to give the tickets away as gifts, I took the chance. It has taken me forever to get the money to pay for them, but that's another story.

I was completely surprised that I was expected to pay for my 3 daughters (ages 3, 4, & 5 yrs old) when I arrived at the premiere. I didn't argue with the young lady though because I know she was just trying to do her job. I told her if she insisted, she could just write my name down and I would add the additional $20 dollars to the amount owed when I pay for the rest of the 10 tickets.

So often people in the church miss the whole point of why they are doing, or suppose to be doing what they are doing. "Free" is supposed to be the bases for all that we do as workers in the Kingdom of GOD, but so many has attached a price to everything that is done concerning the Gospel, that it is shameful. We all know that everything has a cost attached to it, and those expenses need to be covered or the project won't be able to continue. But I'm a firm believer that when it comes to the Gospel of JESUS CHRIST, if a person wants admittance to an event put on by a Ministry and they don't have the money, they should be allowed to get in free without giving it any thought…but that's just how I see it.

When I the LORD opens the door for the very first real event hosted by JAMMIN4JESUS productions, that's the rule I shall apply. A price will be set, but if the person don't have the money to pay to get in, just can't afford it at the time, or just don't want to pay the price, they will still be allowed admittance. I will ask that a name & number be given so that it will bear record of the position taken by them, or the reason for the "not paying", and this information will be used to follow up with the patron later.

November 2, 2013…Sunday 11:00am Service

I was a little late getting there (in spite of the extra hour we gained the night before), but we made it. My daughters are always excited about going to church, and my prayer is that they always remain excited. I also asked my sister if my nieces were interested in going, but they weren't. Even though I'm called to preached the Gospel, I recognize that everyone is not, and that everyone won't be crazy about church like I may be. This of course is to be expected, especially amongst family, but it still leaves me a bit concern. If we teach our kids to love "things" more than they love GOD, then we are setting them up for a serious problem in Life.

I know my daughters are very young, but they have always loved going to church; they know about GOD/JESUS, and they also know that we are suppose to GO to church. I pray with them when they go to bed, say "Grace" when it is time to eat, and PRAY for them always throughout the day & night. And that's part of our responsibility when it comes to raising children. GOD has blessed us with them, and we are require to show some gratitude by teaching them about the "things of GOD" as the HOLY SPIRIT teaches us.

Service was great, and I really felt today's message confirmed yet again that City Church is where I belong. I would even encourage & recommend that today's message be purchased and listen to. So much so, that I may include it in this Book II series. Of course this was a big contrast from just a few minutes earlier when I was driving from Waggaman to get to church. I felt like a stranger, and didn't see the point of driving all the way from Waggaman just to be at City Church while "my Life" was so crazy... In need of a place to live with my daughters, driving a car that's not sure if it wants to continue to transport me and my kids back and forth from work & school, and being robbed by a system so crooked that I could scream. But after service I realized that I wouldn't feel like a stranger if I wouldn't allow myself to be distracted by "things". When things are crazy, this is when we should be running to church, but instead we often stop going because we don't see the point. And seeing others that we know aren't living right, and don't care nothing about trying to please GOD, seeing them doing better then you are, sure doesn't help. But over the years I've learn to ignore the "wicked" cause I know it's just a matter of time before the "gravel drops" and the judgment of GOD falls…and the wicked is…no more.

All my girls went to "children's church" and no one cried; Jayla was even excited about going. Usually when I would try and convince her to go in the room, she didn't want no part of it. She wasn't going to leave Daddy's side, and wasn't entertaining any suggestions. Now today, she gladly strolls into the kid's church with her sisters Jasmine and Janiyah . So I got to hear the "Word of GOD" without the usual interruption of,

"Daddy I got to pee";

"Daddy hold me";

Or, "nope don't go to sleep, I need ya'll to stay awake".

(S T O P)...unscheduled interruption

If you notice the last entry in this Book II, you'll see that the date was November 2, 2013. As I make this entry, the actual date is September 12, 2014...almost a year later. So much has happen since my last entry in this book; some of it good, some of it bad. I know there is no way for me to try and remember all that have occurred in these past 10 months in Chronological order, so I'm not going to try. At first I was going to abandon this Project, and stop at two Books instead of the four I'd plan to write in this series. But I'm going to continue (LORD willing) and hope I can survive the writing of the next two. I won't say much here about the last 10 months of my life, and I'm sorry that I don't have all the "juicy" details written down. Since I've decided to start Book III though, I'm going to try to remember the major occurrences of the past 10 months, and include a lot of the details in Book III. I'll say this much about the past 10 months; at the moment I'm sitting in a 10x10 storage facility making this entry. And it's only by the grace of GOD that I can because my other lap-top started "tripping" and wouldn't work right a long time ago. Partly why I couldn't continue Book II, and have this major gap in the entry dates.

Also, my storage facility doubles as my office in the day, and the place where I sleep at night. Other times, I sleep in my car.

Yea I have lots of sister & brother, and you might wonder why I don't stay with my family. Well, I'm sure many of you already know that family is sometimes more difficult to live with than friends. And since I don't have my three daughters with me, it is no big deal for me to sleep in my car under the stars.

Where are my girls you ask?

Their crazy-ass (yes I did say "ass"…the shoe fits too well) mother stole them and took them back to Texas. That's another story I'll include in Book III.

I still haven't found a job since being force to quit the last "crazy" one. Yes I quit; let's just say I prayed, got my answer, and didn't go back after lunch. I'll leave those details for Book III as well. I was bless to get unemployment; $84 a week. It ain't much but I eat, get to wash my clothes, have a cheap phone for job searching, and I can pay for my 10x10 storage at $85 a month. Overall, I'm surviving. I haven't seen or heard from girls since April when they were snatch in the last part of their schooling. But I don't worry about that either; GOD don't sleep. Had the nerve to call and ask me for money 3 days ago; hadn't heard from my kids in almost 6 months. Ho (yes I called her one…I could have called her worse) must be out of her mind. Two years ago she was sneaking out my house at 2am dragging my kids with her to meet some nigga (yea I said it…whorish nigga) she met on Facebook while I worked the 7p-7a shift at the hospital?

She better look to that sorry-ass nigga to give her some money (yea I said it again).

Lied and had me thrown in jail after I won custody of my kids? Then snatched them from me a second time?

...sounds like she better have a better plan than looking to me for money. She can kiss my dairy ire... (Didn't say what I wanted to; might as well since the LORD know it was said anyway in my mind); lesson for the babe Christian.

Well I guess I better end Book II, since this subject is turning me into that "Angry Black Man" I used to know. GOD knows I don't need a visit from "him"...things my get ugly and somebody this time WILL get mutilated (yea, that's the word I meant...hurt would be letting them get off to easy).

12 Months From Now/Book II

Well before I go, let me mentioned the good things that have happen...

I finally got my partially owned truck fix, and have gone to church the last two Sundays in a row. Even got baptized again; last Sunday, 5 days ago. That's another story I'll save for Book III also; it has to do with a dream the Lord showed me.

Also, I finally finished another book. I'm trying to get it printed in the next 30 days. Book I is done; Book II is now done (when I finish this entry); and I have one more Book to complete. The goal is to get all five books to the printer to be coming off the press in the next 30 days. I've had my own Publishing business for the past 25 years, but just never been able to get it up and running. Was always too busy raising my family; but isn't that's what I was supposed to do?

Been searching forever since I've been back home, and I finally found a house that

Is ME; awaiting GOD's approval. I'm also waiting on the ok on the one in Texas (the house is so ME), and possible one in Alabama. The main house is here though because this is where the LORD said HE wanted me to be.

…So that's what's been happening in my life. It's a crazy life, but I never wanted a boring simple one.

Oh yea! I forgot to mention the song I believe the LORD gave me: it's a doozie! Lyrics are finish; melody is finish, now I'm just trying to schedule with my friend and get the video done.

I need to bring this entry to a close. I've been writing since yesterday morning, and it is now 9:45 at night. I slept from 5am to 8:30am, had a little microwave Ramekin noodles a few hours ago, watch it pour down raining about 5 pm, and then took a 20 minute stroll on the Levee. Overall, it's been a productive day. The book I finally finished turned out really well. I'm very happy with the ending. It's about a Ghost; it should be out for Halloween.

Be bless!

…I'm ya boy "SIR…the SOULman"; Got to get some sleep. Maybe one day we'll meet…Adios! My friends…y va con DIOS!

+   +   +

Date: SEPTEMBER 12, 2014…Time: 10:03pm

...THE END

"12 MONTHS FROM NOW..."

Book II

(As you can see, the original 12 months has long ended: but let's see what GOD wants to do from here on)

| 12 Months From Now/Book II

www.ingramcontent.com/pod-product-compliance
Lightning Source LLC
Chambersburg PA
CBHW061448040426
42450CB00007B/1275